Your New IDENTITY

How to Live as a Child of God

Kim Wampler-Hill

Your New Identity

Copyright ©2023 by Kim Wampler-Hill

No part of this book may be reproduced without permission from the publisher or copyright holder who holds the copyright, except for a reviewer who may quote brief passages in a review; nor may any part of this book be transmitted in any form or by any means, electronic, mechanical, photocopying, recording, or other means without prior written permission from the publisher or copyright holder.

Unless otherwise noted, all Scriptures are taken from The Holy Bible, Modern English Version. Copyright © 2014 by Military Bible Association. Published and distributed by Charisma House.

Scriptures marked (NIV) are taken from The Holy Bible, New International Version®, NIV® Copyright ©1973, 1978, 1984, 2011 by Biblica, Inc.® Used by permission. All rights reserved worldwide.

Published by HigherLife Development Services Inc.
PO Box 623307
Oviedo, Florida 32762
www.ahigherlife.com

REL012000, RELIGION / Christian Living / General
REL012120, RELIGION / Christian Living / Spiritual Growth
REL023000, RELIGION / Christian Living / Discipleship

ISBN: 978-1-958211-57-1 (paperback)
ISBN: 978-1-958211-65-6 (hardback)
ISBN: 978-1-958211-66-3 (ebook)

Library of Congress Control Number: 2023911132

Printed in the United States of America.

10 9 8 7 6 5 4 3 2 1

This book is dedicated to my paternal grandmother, Alpha C. Lusk, who prayed with me as a toddler and for me as I grew; who led her life by Christian example and was a strong link in a family chain under generational blessings.

Contents

Introduction 1
Chapter 1 - A Sinner No More 5
Chapter 2 - A New Creature 11
Chapter 3 - Chosen 19
Chapter 4 - Fruit 25
Chapter 5 - Fire 35
Chapter 6 - The Cross 39
Chapter 7 - The Trinity 51
Chapter 8 - Relationship 53
Chapter 9 - Praise 59
Chapter 10 - Armor 65
Chapter 11 - Prayer 69
Chapter 12 - Names of God 73
Chapter 13 - Maturity in Christ 79
Chapter 14 - Power 83
Chapter 15 - Sanctification 85
Chapter 16 - The Great Commission 91
Conclusion 95

I have fed you with milk and not with solid food. For to this day, you were not able to endure it. Nor are you able now.

(1 Corinthians 3:2)

Acknowledgments

First and foremost, I thank my Lord, Jesus Christ, for choosing to partner with me in this project and for providing the inspiration and passion for the content.

I also thank my mom for choosing life and the difficult path of motherhood that allowed me to be raised knowing my family. For teaching me the value of telling the truth and of appreciating and caring for the world around me. And for the many sacrifices that came with the responsibility.

Thanks also go to my dad for the fatherly love that he has given me. For supporting me consistently with the message that I can do anything that I set my mind to. For speaking words of blessing over me. For showing me by example to lend my help and lift people up when I can.

To my husband, Russell, deepest thanks for standing behind me in everything I do. For keeping me grounded and lifting me up. For being the voice of reason when I am unreasonable. For walking with me and being my partner. For endless love and encouragement.

I thank my grandmothers, who were always there to provide stability, unconditional love, and to foster tradition and wisdom in my life.

My two aunts, although so very young themselves, were always there to enhance my life with experiences and to give me the love and support of family. Thank you both.

I want to thank my "stepdad," Bill, for being such a strong figure in my early, formative years. For being one more voice teaching me right from wrong and for bringing music into my life.

Thanks also to my stepmom, Renette (Renee), who for many years provided me a picture of what a godly woman and marriage looked like. For taking me to church with her and being such a strong part and primary influence in my walk with God for so many years.

To my first pastor, Lonnie Snow, thanks for drumming into my head the power of my words and laying a firm foundation of faith that I continue to build on today.

I thank my current pastor, Thomas Humphries ("Pastor T"), for teaching the Bible and the Word of God without compromise.

Last but not least, I would like to thank the publishing team at HigherLife Publishing and my project manager, Paul Renfroe, who made the process easy and smooth.

Introduction

This book is intended as an introduction for a new believer to a life of walking with Christ. The inspiration for writing it comes from seeing people throughout the years say the prayer of salvation and then seemingly step back into their old lives. As followers of Christ, we are meant to be set apart. The Bible calls us a peculiar people. We are no longer a part of this fallen world, but temporary residents until we reach our eternal home. For this reason, our lives really should look and feel different.

So, what has happened if we don't notice a change after our conversion? Perhaps some fail to recognize the full extent of the prayer of salvation. More likely, it is just that it takes time before we recognize our transformation. In fact, it may be those around us who notice the changes first.

We believe. We confess. We make Jesus the Lord of our lives. What does that mean? What should it look like? Hopefully, within the subjects of this book we can follow up on your initial commitment and shed some light on how to pursue your newly found life. Or at least it will be a starting point. I pray you find some nourishment for your roots to feed on as they spread and grow.

I believe that God's heart for this book is to escalate growth in His people. Many will be coming to the Lord during the great harvest that we are stepping into, and He wants us to be prepared for such a time as this. We are blessed to be a part of this chapter in His story. We are chosen to be right here at this moment in time. As the time until Christ's return shortens, He needs workers. The work is plentiful, and the workers are few. There is work to be done!!

> He said to them, "The harvest truly is plentiful, but the laborers are few. Pray therefore the Lord of the harvest to send out laborers into His harvest." (Luke 10:2)

You will see Bible verses to support the discussion points in this book. I would encourage you to go to the Bible and read the entire chapter or book to gain the full context of what is being said. Look for depth and revelation in what God is saying directly to you within the content. The Bible is full of living, breathing words. Let it speak to you, let it teach you, let it guide your life. Take a verse; meditate on it. This is how we grow and develop. You will eat of the knowledge and

Introduction

become hungry for more. You will begin to crave it until you are devouring it day and night.

The verses in this book were pulled from the Modern English Version (MEV) of the Bible with a few exceptions in cases where another version best brought out the revelation of the subject matter for the book.

All praise to the Lord our God for His love, His correction, and His constant revelations.

Chapter 1

A Sinner No More

> For God so loved the world that He gave His only begotten Son, that whoever believes in Him should not perish, but have eternal life. (John 3:16)

So, you said the "sinner's prayer." In doing so, you have confessed with your mouth, "Jesus is Lord," and you believe in your heart that God raised Him (Jesus) from the dead (Romans 10:9). Now Jesus says of you, "Whoever will confess Me before men, him will I confess also before My Father who is in heaven" (Matthew 10:32).

> Come to Me, all you who labor and are heavily burdened, and I will give you rest. (Matthew 11:28)

> All whom the Father gives Me will come to Me, and he who comes to Me I will never cast out. (John 6:37)

Your New IDENTITY

So, what does it mean that Jesus is now your Lord? Lord is the name we call God when we are referring to His position of authority and leadership over our lives. A common definition of Lord is someone having power, authority, or influence. When we call Jesus Lord, we are submitting to Him. Submitting to His authority. Submitting to His correction. Submitting to His direction. We are no longer "gods" of our own minds and of our own lives. We are making Him our God. His way is perfect and sovereign. He is always faithful to His Word.

> *When we call Jesus "Lord," we are submitting to Him.*

> For you have been born again, not of perishable seed but imperishable, through the word of God which lives and abides forever. (1 Peter 1:23)

> Come now, and let us reason together, says the Lord. Though your sins be as scarlet, they shall be as white as snow; though they be red like crimson, they shall be as wool. (Isaiah 1:18)

In Reinhard Bonnke's book *Living a Life of Fire* (more on fire later), he refers to the ABCs of Salvation.

Admit (that you are a sinner in need of salvation).

Believe (that Christ came to earth to die and rise from the dead to cleanse you of your sins).

Confess (with your mouth that Jesus Christ is your salvation and the Lord of your life).

There is no other prerequisite for accepting this gift of redemption. God calls us and wants us to choose Him with our free will. God is a God of freedom, after all. And who would want to be followed by force or coercion? Our God is no tyrant.

> The Lord is not slow concerning His promise, as some men count slowness; but He is patient with us, because He does not want any to perish, but all to come to repentance. (2 Peter 3:9)
>
> As free people, do not use your liberty as a covering for evil, but live as servants of God. (1 Peter 2:16)

Sometimes we hear discussion and even debate among those in the body of Christ about "once saved, always saved." Can you lose salvation once you receive it? Since we cannot do anything to earn it for ourselves, can this gift that Jesus gave us be taken away? If we are saved and that is the end of story, what is a backslidden

Christian? It is a complex subject to say the least, one into which I have put a lot of thought. There are Bible passages that can be pulled as evidence by both sides of the debate. Otherwise, it would not be such a matter of discussion within the body of Christ. Who can answer this but God Himself? Who knows our hearts better than He does? What we do know is that the Bible says that His grace is sufficient for us. We also see that He is long-suffering. Each of us must evaluate our own condition, based on our walk as a believer and our personal connection to God.

If there comes a time that you find yourself wondering where you stand in your salvation, you may as well begin to examine your life and why the question is coming up. It may just be a prompting of the Holy Spirit nudging to get you back on your path.

If you are thinking, "Hey, that is not an answer," well ... you are right. How can man truly judge the heart and motivation of someone else? However, as new creatures, we have Him dwelling inside us and leading us. The Holy Spirit provides clues for discernment, such as in the visible fruits of the Spirit working (or not working) in our lives and the lives of others ... so that we can recognize where there may be struggle, and be prompted to prayer.

Praise God for His grace and endless mercy, and glory to Him who sits on the throne.

> Therefore, my beloved, as you have always obeyed, not only in my presence, but so much more in my absence, work out your salvation with fear and trembling. For God is the One working in you, both to will and to do His good pleasure. (Philippians 2:12–13)

Chapter 2

A New Creature

> Therefore, if any man is in Christ, he is a new creature. Old things have passed away. Look, all things have become new. (2 Corinthians 5:17)

As a born-again believer, a baby Christian, a new creature in Christ Jesus, you have a fresh start! A new lease on life! A hope for eternity! A new family! A friend, confidant, lover, and savior in Jesus Christ!

You are comprised in three parts (yes, much like the trinity itself). As such, we are a SPIRIT who possesses a SOUL and lives in a BODY.

Our spirit is unseen by the natural eye. Everyone, lost or found, has a spirit. This explains why we can sometimes think of someone just before they call us on the phone, or we see them in person. As a believer, our spirit is redeemed and is one with the Holy Spirit. In fact, He dwells within us. Our spirit is the part of us that is connected to the Spirit of God, the Holy Spirit.

Your New IDENTITY

As we grow and become closer and more in tune with Him, we will begin to recognize that we can feel, see, and hear in the spirit. The Holy Spirit speaks to our spirit. If we listen and stay in tune, He will prompt us to pray for someone, alert us to unsafe situations, and give us spiritual insight to light our path and guide our feet. In the natural realm, people refer to this when they say something like, "I had a feeling," or "That person made my Spidey senses tingle" (okay, just had to say that). This connection is what might give our body goose bumps in certain situations and speaks to anything that we might call intuition.

Our soul is comprised of our mind, our will, our thoughts, and our feelings. It is the soul that died when separated from God by sin in the garden of Eden. Adam and Eve didn't die physically by that act of rebellion. It separated their (and our) souls from God. That separation is the reason that we are now born to a sinful nature. It began the process of death and separation that we see in the decline of society and morals.

Our soul is where we see the biggest transformation as a new creature in Christ Jesus. This transformation is often referred to as "dying to self," as we transform into the new creature that God has created us to be. During this process, the fruits of the Spirit begin to grow and mature to replace the old worldly self that we were. That old person is gone. We begin to develop the mind of Christ. We will further discuss this when we read about the fruits of the Spirit in the next chapter.

Our body is our physical body. There isn't much explanation needed on this. This physical body begins the process of dying the moment it stops growing ... some say the moment it is born. However, once redeemed, we will one day have a new body. Just as Jesus was resurrected with a new body, our new body will also be resurrected. Our bodies will be glorified: free from pain, sickness, disease, depression, and so many more miseries that these frail and temporal bodies experience in this world. Our bodies will be transformed, just as Jesus' body was glorified when He ascended to be with the Father.

Here is just a sample of who you are now that you are saved and redeemed.

You are a child of God.

> Yet to all who received Him, to them He gave the power to become sons of God, to those who believed in His name. (John 1:12)

You are a branch of the true vine.

> I am the true vine, and My Father is the vinedresser ... I am the vine, you are the

> branches; he who remains in Me and I in him, bears much fruit, for without Me you can do nothing. (John 15:1, 5)

You are a friend of Jesus.

> I no longer call you servants, for a servant does not know what his master does. But I have called you friends, for everything that I have heard from My Father have I made known to you. (John 15:15)

You are justified and redeemed.

> ... being justified freely by His grace through the redemption that is in Christ Jesus. (Romans 3:24)

You are a new creature; your old self was crucified with Christ, and you are no longer a slave to sin.

> ... knowing this, that our old man has been crucified with Him, so that the body of sin might be destroyed, and we should no longer be slaves to sin. (Romans 6:6)

You are free.

> For the law of the Spirit of life in Christ Jesus has set me free from the law of sin and death. (Romans 8:2)

A New Creature

As a child of God, you are a fellow heir with Christ.

> For as many as are led by the Spirit of God, these are the sons of God. For you have not received the spirit of slavery again to fear. But you have received the Spirit of adoption, by whom we cry, "Abba Father." The Spirit Himself bears witness with our spirits that we are the children of God, and if children, then heirs: heirs of God and joint-heirs with Christ, if indeed we suffer with Him, that we may also be glorified with Him. (Romans 8:14–17)

You have been called to be a saint.

> To the church of God which is at Corinth, to those who are sanctified in Christ Jesus, called to be saints, with all who in every place call on the name of Jesus Christ our Lord, both their Lord and ours. (1 Corinthians 1:2; See also Ephesians 1:1; Philippians 1:1; Colossians 1:2)

In Christ Jesus, you have wisdom, righteousness, sanctification, and redemption.

> But because of Him you are in Christ Jesus, whom God made unto us wisdom, righteousness, sanctification, and redemption. (1 Corinthians 1:30)

Your New IDENTITY

Your body is a temple of the Holy Spirit who dwells in you.

> Do you not know that you are the temple of God, and that the Spirit of God dwells in you? ... What? Do you not know that your body is the temple of the Holy Spirit, who is in you, whom you have received from God, and that you are not your own? (1 Corinthians 3:16; 6:19)

You are joined to the Lord and are one spirit with Him.

> But he who is joined to the Lord becomes one spirit with Him. (1 Corinthians 6:17)

God leads you in the triumph and knowledge of Christ.

> Now thanks be to God who always causes us to triumph in Christ and through us reveals the fragrance of His knowledge in every place. (2 Corinthians 2:14)

The hardening of your mind has been removed in Christ.

> Instead, their minds were blinded. For until this day the same veil remains unlifted in the reading of the old covenant, the veil which was done away with in Christ. (2 Corinthians 3:14)

A New Creature

You have become the righteousness of God in Christ.

> God made Him who knew no sin to be sin for us, that we might become the righteousness of God in Him. (2 Corinthians 5:21)

You have been made one with all who are in Christ Jesus.

> There is neither Jew nor Greek, there is neither slave nor free, and there is neither male nor female, for you are all one in Christ Jesus. (Galatians 3:28)

You are blessed.

> Blessed be the God and Father of our Lord Jesus Christ, who has blessed us with every spiritual blessing in the heavenly places in Christ. (Ephesians 1:3)

You are chosen.

> ... just as He chose us in Him before the foundation of the world, to be holy and blameless before Him in love. (Ephesians 1:4)

You are redeemed.

> In Him we have redemption through His blood and the forgiveness of sins according to the riches of His grace. (Ephesians 1:7)

Your New IDENTITY

You are seated in the heavenly places with Christ.

> ... and He raised us up and seated us together in the heavenly places in Christ Jesus. (Ephesians 2:6)

You are God's workmanship.

> For we are His workmanship, created in Christ Jesus for good works, which God prepared beforehand, so that we should walk in them. (Ephesians 2:10)

You are righteous and holy.

> ... put on the new nature, which was created according to God in righteousness and true holiness. (Ephesians 4:24)

You are a citizen of heaven.

> But our citizenship is in heaven, from where also we await for our Savior, the Lord Jesus Christ. (Philippians 3:20)

You are complete in Christ.

> And you are complete in Him, who is the head of all authority and power. (Colossians 2:10)

Praise You, O Lord, for taking us and making us new creatures in You. Let everything that has breath praise the Lord!!

Chapter 3

Chosen

> ... just as He chose us in Him before the foundation of the world, to be holy and blameless before Him in love; He predestined us to adoption as sons to Himself through Jesus Christ according to the good pleasure of His will. (Ephesians 1:4–5)

At one point in my Christian life it was normal practice for me to praise, pray, and spend time with the Lord during my commute. No music, no radio, just me and God. One day, during my commute, the Holy Spirit took me on a journey back through my childhood memories and highlighted for me how the seed of faith was sown into my life, and how it was watered and fertilized through the years.

My earliest memory of God is when my paternal grandmother would pray with me at night before I went to sleep. "I pray the Lord my soul to keep, but if I should die before I awake, I pray the Lord my soul to take." It was simple really. And even though the part

Your New IDENTITY

about dying was a bit scary to a toddler, this memory stands out to me. I can also remember playing with my toys while she watched her morning sermons, Robert Schuller and his *Hour of Power* as well as sermons by John Hagee.

You see, I was born to a fifteen-year-old mother and an eighteen-year-old father. Although they married because of the pregnancy, my father joined the Air Force to avoid the draft in 1969, the year I was born. He remained in England until I was four or five years old, and my mother filed for divorce while he was away. As was probably rare in such a situation and with such a young man, my father remained in my life and I saw him regularly on holidays and spent weeks in the summer with him at his out-of-state home. I lived near his family and they also remained a consistent part of my life.

My mother attended classes, worked a full-time job, and maintained as much of a social life as she could with a toddler at home. My mom was raised in my maternal grandmother's home, and Grandmother was a Jehovah's Witness. Mom attended Jehovah's Witness services as a child and, as the sect prescribed, was not allowed to celebrate birthdays, Christmas, or any other holidays. She had to leave the classroom at school and stand in the hall when the class said the Pledge of Allegiance each day. The same was true with any classroom holiday celebrations. As soon as she was old enough to do so, she completely severed herself from this and any other organized religion. In fact, the only real memory of my mom mentioning God was when she told me that the sound of thunder was actually God bowling in heaven, to ease my young mind in a storm. Home was not where I would learn about the truth of salvation and the love of God.

In first grade, I had a childhood friend with whom I had sleepovers every Saturday night. I began going to Sunday School with her at a Methodist church just four doors down the street from my home. I only attended for a short time in the grand scheme of things, but it represents one of the ways that I was being nurtured and wooed by the Lord.

When I was ten years old, my dad came to town with news of a new wife and stepmom for me. I hadn't met her yet, but she was pregnant with my baby brother. News of a new baby brother delighted me and made this an exciting announcement. My dad was only about twenty-eight at the time, and his new wife was twenty. I was a single child, and the only grandchild who lived locally to my grandparents. I was okay with having my dad all to myself, and Dad's new wife was not used to being a stepmom. Not only that, but I'd really liked his previous girlfriend. Needless to say, this adjustment took time for all concerned. But soon that new baby came along, I became a big sister, and that was just fine with me.

I continued to visit my dad's house in another state during the summer and it turned out that my stepmom was a Christian. Again I look back and see God's hand in my life. She went to a non-denominational church and she was glad for me to ride along. I looked forward to the church services. I went to the altar for the prayer of salvation, I was baptized with the Holy Spirit, and I was so excited for all of all of it. My stepmom researched to find a non-denominational church in my hometown that I might attend. But the truth is, it just didn't happen. The church was across town from my home, and who would take me on a regular basis? Church attendance fell by the wayside except when I was visiting my dad each year, when I would attend with my stepmom and work in the nursery at her church during my brief visits. She may never know the impact she had on my life. She was my first real Christian role model and remained such for many years.

Soon boys, music, teenage interests, and school life distracted me from my faith for several years. I married my high school sweetheart at seventeen just after finding out we were going to have a baby. Before we were married, my husband would drop me off at his cousin's house to hang out with his wife while they would run around and play basketball. She and I hit it off and became inseparable friends. She was raised in a Christian home and, in fact, her father was a pastor and conducted the wedding ceremony when I was married.

When I was twenty years old, I began attending a church full time in my home town. I attended regularly, up to three services a week, volunteered in the nursery, and eventually worked full time at the daycare alongside the friend I mentioned above. After a few years the pastors moved on to seed a church in another state. I tried for a while to stay on at the church under the new pastor, but it wasn't the same and so my attendance dwindled. My beliefs and certainty in the Lord remained, but without a home church, I slid into a lukewarm state.

When I was twenty-nine, my husband and I divorced. By this time, we had three children together. Although I would attend church from time to time, I was living in a backslidden state. Even so, I never stopped believing, I never stopped praying, and I never actually stopped confessing my beliefs when the subject came up. But I was not on the path that God had for me. I was not open to His correction in my life. I was presuming on His grace and mercy. It took about twenty years of walking on my own path before I fully turned back to the Lord.

The point is, He chose me. He had wooed me and saved me and was not going to leave me on my own in the wilderness. His grace was there gently pointing me back to Him. His arms were open to me when I returned. He did not forsake me.

> *He chose me. He had wooed me and saved me and was not going to leave me on my own in the wilderness.*

Everyone's story is unique and everyone's path is entirely different. There is darkness in the untold part of my story. There is guilt, condemnation, and burden. He has brought me so far, and I have so much further to go.

Thank You, my dear Lord, for calling me, for that soft, gentle whisper as You guided me into the safety of Your wings.

Chapter 4

Fruit

> A good tree does not bear corrupt fruit, nor does a corrupt tree bear good fruit. Each tree is known by its own fruit. Men do not gather figs from thorns, nor do they gather grapes from a wild bush. (Luke 6:43–44)

> Can the fig tree, my brothers, bear olives, or a vine, figs? So no spring can yield both salt water and fresh water. (James 3:12)

The fruits of the Spirit are the evidence of the Holy Spirit's influence on believers as we grow in our unique role as a part of the body of Christ. The Word of God names love, joy, peace, patience, kindness, goodness, faithfulness, gentleness, and self-control as the fruits of the Spirit.

When we begin to see others through the eyes of God, our perspective changes. As a part of the body of Christ, we begin to have the heart of Christ. We see others as Christ sees them. We begin to recognize the pain behind anger. We see the insecurity that has built defensive walls. We see the past hurts that have calloused and hardened hearts. We begin to see others as children in need of love and truth. We see sweet souls longing for the hope that can only come through salvation. We see all this in love and compassion. We begin to love others as Jesus loves them. Our eyes are opened wide as we begin to develop the fruits of the Spirit.

As believers, we are identified by the fruit that we produce in our lives. Once we are born again, we become fruitful in our lives, behaviors, relationships, and reactions. Our very minds and hearts have been transformed. Once transformed, we are not the same. The changes may come slowly as we grow closer to Christ, or radically and in an instant. Either way, a true believer will produce good fruit. This transformation is the outward evidence of the change that has taken place in us. Observing these fruits in others allows us to discern the godly confidants, teachers, and models who will help us in our Christian journey.

> You will know them by their fruit. Do men gather grapes from thorns, or figs from thistles? Even so, every good tree bears good fruit. But a corrupt tree bears evil fruit. A good tree cannot bear evil fruit, nor can a corrupt tree bear good fruit. (Matthew 7:16–18)

These traits don't require much explanation. The fruits are, in fact, words that we hear time and again as part of our everyday lives, even before becoming believers. The fruits of the Spirit <u>do not</u> represent weakness, low stature, vulnerability to harm, or a victim mentality. In fact, there is strength and confidence in every aspect of the traits found in these fruits.

It takes strength to love someone who does not appear to be loveable or who does not treat you with love. It takes strength to find joy in the middle of the trials in our lives. It takes peace and patience when the enemy is using a person or situation against you. And it takes strength to be faithful and maintain self-control in the face of temptation. And how many of these traits are we using when we forgive and pray for those who have hurt or wronged us deeply?

> *There is absolutely no weakness to be found in walking in the fruits of the Spirit, not by our own might, but by His strength within us.*

It also takes strength to forgive. Although forgiveness is not specifically outlined as a fruit, Scripture does make it clear that we are to forgive. And I think it is fair to say that it is a byproduct of the fruits of the

Spirit. It takes love, peace, kindness, and goodness to forgive. And lack of forgiveness eats us from the inside out. Is it even possible to walk in the fruits of the Spirit while carrying the heavy load of unforgiveness?

> For if you forgive other people when they sin against you, your heavenly Father will also forgive you. But if you do not forgive others their sins, your Father will not forgive your sins. (Matthew 6:14–15 NIV)

There is absolutely no weakness to be found in walking in the fruits of the Spirit, not by our own might, but by His strength within us. All glory to God.

> But the fruit of the Spirit, is love, joy, peace, patience, gentleness, goodness, faith, meekness, and self-control; against such there is no law. (Galatians 5:22–23)

Love

> Honor all people. Love the brotherhood. Fear God. Honor the king. (1 Peter 2:17)

> Love suffers long and is kind; love envies not; love flaunts not itself and is not puffed up, does not behave itself improperly, seeks not its own, is not easily provoked, thinks no evil; rejoices not in iniquity, but rejoices in the truth; bears all

Fruit

things, believes all things, hopes all things, and endures all things. (1 Corinthians 13:4–7)

So now abide faith, hope, and love, these three. But the greatest of these is love. (1 Corinthians 13:13)

Joy

Rejoice always, pray without ceasing. In everything give thanks, for this is the will of God in Christ Jesus concerning you. (1 Thessalonians 5:16–18)

Rejoice in the Lord always. Again I will say, rejoice! (Philippians 4:4)

You will make known to me the path of life; in Your presence is fullness of joy; at Your right hand there are pleasures for evermore. (Psalm 16:11)

Peace

Do not fear, for I am with you; do not be dismayed, for I am your God. (Isaiah 41:10)

Turn away from evil, and do good; seek peace, and pursue it. (Psalm 34:14)

> Be therefore merciful, even as your Father is merciful. (Luke 6:36)

Patience

> With all humility, meekness, and patience, bearing with one another in love, be eager to keep the unity of the Spirit in the bond of peace. (Ephesians 4:2–3)

> But if we hope for what we do not see, we wait for it with patience. (Romans 8:25)

> Wait on the Lord; be strong, and may your heart be stout; wait on the Lord. (Psalm 27:14)

Kindness

> A soft answer turns away wrath, but grievous words stir up anger. (Proverbs 15:1)

> But I say to you that for every idle word that men speak, they will give an account on the Day of Judgment. (Matthew 12:36)

> And be kind to one another, tenderhearted, forgiving one another, just as God in Christ also forgave you. (Ephesians 4:32)

Goodness

> Let your light so shine before men that they may see your good works and glorify your Father who is in heaven. (Matthew 5:16)

> Therefore, as we have opportunity, let us do good to all people, especially to those who are of the household of faith. (Galatians 6:10)

> Do not be overcome by evil, but overcome evil with good. (Romans 12:21)

> Who is he who will harm you if you follow that which is good? (1 Peter 3:13)

Faithfulness

> You who love the Lord, hate evil! He preserves the lives of His devoted ones; He delivers them from the hand of the wicked. (Psalm 97:10)

> But the mercy of the Lord is from everlasting to everlasting upon those who fear Him, and His righteousness to children's children, to those who keep His covenant, and to those who remember to do His commandments. (Psalm 103:17–18)

Your New IDENTITY

> Watch therefore, for you do not know what hour your Lord will come. (Matthew 24:42)

> Because iniquity will abound, the love of many will grow cold. But he who endures to the end shall be saved. (Matthew 24:12–13)

> Look, I am coming quickly. Hold firmly what you have, so that no one may take your crown. (Revelation 3:11)

Gentleness

> A wholesome tongue is a tree of life, but perverseness in it crushes the spirit. (Proverbs 15:4)

> Let your speech always be with grace, seasoned with salt, that you may know how you should answer everyone. (Colossians 4:6)

Self-Control

> *Therefore, lay aside all filthiness and remaining wickedness and receive with meekness the engrafted word, which is able to save your souls. (James 1:21)*

> If anyone among you seems to be religious and does not bridle his tongue, but deceives

Fruit

his own heart, this man's religion is vain.
(James 1:26)

For God has not given us a spirit of fear, but of power, and love, and self-control.
(2 Timothy 1:7)

Dear Lord, prune me, make me to bear sweet, delicious fruit to nourish and bless Your people that I might be a joy and delight to You.

Chapter 5

Fire

> I indeed baptize you with water to repentance, but He who is coming after me is mightier than I, whose shoes I am not worthy to carry. He will baptize you with the Holy Spirit and with fire.
> (Matthew 3:11)

We commonly hear about water baptism. We have seen it in movies and television programs. Water baptism is familiar in our culture as an outward act and sign of commitment to our rebirth in Christ. But how often do we hear about baptism with fire? It is less commonly spoken of and somewhat less understood. We see water baptism in our churches all the time; regardless of denomination, water baptisms are common practice. But how often do we see and hear about baptism with fire? John the Baptist refers to it and, in fact, differentiates it from the water baptisms that he was known for. Baptism in the Holy Spirit is what is referred to as baptism with fire.

> I baptize with water but One stands among you, whom you do not know. (John 1:26)
>
> I did not know him, but He who sent me to baptize with water said to me, "The One on whom you see the Spirit descending and remaining, this is He who baptizes with the Holy Spirit." (John 1:33)
>
> When the day of Pentecost had come, they were all together in one place. Suddenly a sound like a mighty rushing wind came from heaven, and it filled the whole house where they were sitting. There appeared to them tongues as of fire, being distributed and resting on each of them, and they were all filled with the Holy Spirit and began to speak in other tongues, as the Spirit enabled them to speak. (Acts 2:1–4)
>
> For John baptized with water, but you shall be baptized with the Holy Spirit not many days from now. (Acts 1:5)

When Jesus was risen, resurrected, glorified, and ready to ascend to be with the Father, He told the disciples that it was better for them that He go. How could that be? How in the world could we be better off without

Fire

Jesus here with us on this earth!? He went on to explain this to the disciples. He told them that He must leave so that His people could have something better to help us with our walk on this earth. If it were not so, Jesus would not have said it.

> But the Counselor, the Holy Spirit, whom the Father will send in My name, will teach you everything and remind you of all that I told you. (John 14:26)

Jesus left so that the Holy Spirit could come. Our Helper, our Comforter, our Advocate, to light our paths and to guide our feet. He ushered in the baptism with fire, baptism in the Holy Spirit.

> Peter said to them, "Repent and be baptized, every one of you, in the name of Jesus Christ for the forgiveness of sins, and you shall receive the gift of the Holy Spirit." (Acts 2:38)

Baptism by fire can no longer be a side thought in the church. Regardless of denomination, believers need baptism by fire. The disciples were believers, but they needed to be baptized by the Holy Spirit to continue their

We need the Holy Spirit to help bring in the great harvest that is imminent, that even now is upon us.

walk after Jesus ascended from this earth. We need this in order to endure through the coming times. We need the Holy Spirit to help bring in the great harvest that is imminent, that even now is upon us. We need to seek the Lord and accept this gift of baptism by fire. It was not intended for us to walk through the trials of this world alone.

Dear Father, let Your fire burn in my life. Let it burn through everything in me that is not holy, and let those things fall away like ashes. Let the example of Jesus and the voice of the Holy Spirit flow in and fill me with the loving obedience that best serves my life and the plans You have for me.

Let that fire ignite my heart with the passions that honor You and deepen our love and relationship. Replace my worldly passions for holy passions and my carnal heart with the heart of Jesus.

Let my ways honor You and give You glory so that when others see me, they see You.

Blessed be Your name forever. In the name of Yeshua, Amen.

Chapter 6

The Cross

> But he was wounded for our transgressions, he was bruised for our iniquities; the chastisement of our peace was upon him, and by his stripes we are healed. (Isaiah 53:5)

Christ endured and accomplished so much through His death on the cross. His blood was the ultimate sacrifice, ending humanity's need to make blood sacrifice and offerings for cleansing from sins. He moved us from the rule of law into a new era of grace, love, and mercy. He tore the veil in the temple, giving us direct access to God through Himself. He conquered death and hell. He gave us access to an abundant life here on earth and eternal abundance and life evermore. We have access to healing, deliverance, and wholeness in the here and now. Through Jesus we have access to deep inner peace amidst a world of uncertainty.

Sin: Iniquities and Transgressions

Sin is made up of transgressions and iniquities. Both are born from the sinful nature of a man who is separated from God. Sin became the nature of man when Adam and Eve rebelled and were disobedient to God's instruction in the Garden of Eden. Without the work of Jesus on the cross, we would be forever separated from God. Not because of His will, but because He is pure and good and holy. In our fallen, natural state, we sin every day and are far from being pure, truly good, and holy. Every time we judge someone else's behavior, every time we lose our temper, gossip, behave out of pride or unforgiveness or selfishness, we sin. We simply cannot help it. It is impossible for us in our fallen state to walk in perfect goodness and holiness in this world. Added to this, the enemy is working day and night to knock us off our upward path and put stumbling blocks in our way.

But our separation from God is not only due to Satan's schemes and our inherited fallen state. Without the blood of Jesus to continually wash us clean, our personal sins, our own iniquities and transgressions, lead to the same place: eternal separation from our Creator. Scripture differentiates between transgressions and iniquities and so it is only fitting that we do so as well.

The Cross

> But he (Jesus) was wounded for our transgressions, he was bruised for our iniquities; the chastisement of our peace was upon him, and by his stripes we are healed. All of us like sheep have gone stray; each of us has turned to his own way, but the LORD has laid on him the iniquity of us all. (Isaiah 53:5–6)

Transgressions represent the breaking of a rule or statute. We are committing a transgression when we disregard authority, especially that of God. An example of an act of transgression would be breaking one of God's commandments or breaking one of man's laws.

> *Transgressions represent the breaking of a rule or statute.*

> Blessed is he whose transgression is forgiven, whose sin is covered. Blessed is the man against whom the LORD does not count iniquity, and in whose spirit there is no deceit. (Psalm 32:1–2)

Iniquities are deeply rooted and passed from generation to generation. They may come in the form of substance abuse, physical abuse, pride, unforgiveness, anger issues, depression, and with countless other faces. Iniquities might begin in a family with one individual developing a habit of sin. You hear this referred to: "It runs in the family.... The apple doesn't fall far from the tree.... They are just like their father (or mother)." Iniquities are acts rooted in the evil nature of humanity.

> I acknowledged my sin to You, and my iniquity
> I did not conceal. I said, "I will confess my
> transgressions to the LORD." And You forgave
> the iniquity of my sin. (Psalm 32:5)

Transgressions and iniquities have consequences. I believe that part of the reason that Scripture differentiates between them is that we need to recognize what we are dealing with in order to deal with it in our lives. These sins wreak havoc in our lives. And believers are not immune to consequences of unrepented sin.

Iniquities are acts rooted in the evil nature of humanity.

The good news is that Jesus' blood spilled at the cross freed us from all our sins, whether transgressions or iniquities. That is certainly good. But what else did He accomplish that day?

Infirmity

Jesus' sacrifice on the cross brings the gift of healing just as surely as it brings the gift of salvation. It is just often easier for us to have faith in the latter. God is the same yesterday, today, and always. Jesus demonstrated healing throughout His ministry. He said, "*Truly, truly I say to you, he who believes in Me will do the works that I do also. And he will do greater works than these, because I am going to My Father*" (John 14:12). Who can argue with the words of Christ Himself?

> For I will restore health to you, and I will heal you of your wounds, says the Lord.
> (Jeremiah 30:17)

In 2021 my dad was hospitalized due to illness. As you know, during that time so many were hospitalized with their loved ones unable to be by their side to hold their hands, pray with them, and keep them. My dad is a healthy, strong, active man and was a youthful sixty-nine years old at the time. In fact, he had his seventieth birthday during his hospital stay. He is a man who exercises, eats organic food, and tends to his health in a very purposeful manner.

On October 21 I received a call from him requesting my husband and me to come by and walk his dogs, as he had been under the weather and didn't have the energy to walk them. When we got to the house, he met us at the door, fully dressed and appearing just as always. We walked the dogs and I let him know that we were going for a long weekend away, so we wouldn't be available to walk them over that time. When we returned, I had no reason to believe that there was anything to be concerned about. Then I received a call from one of his life-long friends who said she was concerned, as he'd let on that he was feeling pretty bad, and then she'd not been able to reach him for some days. I spoke to my son, who said that he'd been walking the dogs over the weekend, but that he'd not really seen my dad, who had remained in bed. So, my husband and I went to check on him. I immediately noted that Dad's situation had deteriorated and called an ambulance. The paramedics made it clear that he needed to get some fluids and that his vitals were concerning. This was our first attempt to get him to the hospital, but he was unwilling to go. This was October 25.

We continued to help with the dogs and to take him liquids and anything he needed. I was happy when he asked for homemade split pea soup. Maybe his appetite was returning and this was a sign that he would be on the uptick. So I made him some soup, and when I arrived at his place with it, he told me he was ready to go to the hospital, but that he wanted to go to the VA or another hospital rather than our local one. Unfortunately, the ambulance paramedics said that his vitals were too dangerous to go anywhere but the very closest hospital. When we arrived, I was thankful that I was able to sit with him in the ER room.

The Cross

They set about quickly taking blood and then getting him on fluids. As his symptoms appeared to be digestive issues, we were very surprised to be told at the ER that he'd tested positive for COVID-19 and was in renal failure. This set about a sequence of events that left me feeling utterly helpless for him. You see, we'd wound up at the ER of a hospital to which none of us wanted him admitted. When I told the staff that we did not want my dad admitted, just stabilized enough to transport to the VA hospital, they basically told me, "Too late, we have admitted him." I can remember the sinking feeling I had, standing at the elevator eye to eye with Dad as they took him to his room. I felt so completely helpless and that I was somehow handing him over to the dark. This may sound dramatic, but it is no exaggeration. He was completely awake and lucid during this time in the ER. This was October 27.

The first call I received from the hospital was from palliative care, asking me questions about a DNR (Do Not Resuscitate) and other considerations. "What in the world?" I thought. "He is coming home. This conversation is not appropriate for our situation." I was angry, ... but polite. For days I struggled to get information and updates from the hospital. They gave my concerns very little consideration and the shift nurses in his unit seemed annoyed by my update requests and calls; each shift had a different story about what was going on with him. I continued to persevere in my requests to have him moved to another hospital in a nearby city where my daughter worked as a respiratory therapist in the COVID unit. I also continued to pray and to speak life and recovery over him. During this time, his cell phone had lost its charge, and it took several attempts to get the nurses to put it on the charger I had dropped off. So, I had no way to know his state of mind, or to learn from him what was going on. Finally, once his phone was charged, I began receiving frantic phone calls and texts from him telling me, "Please get me out of here," and "They are killing me." You see, there can be a side effect from certain steroids: steroid delirium. It happened that he had this reaction. This only elevated my helpless feelings and urgency to have him moved.

I reached out to the physician assigned to him and began to use strong language, indicating that they were holding him without our consent. I was a squeaky wheel. Finally, I called and learned that he was in transit, late on a Sunday night, to the hospital where my daughter worked. By the grace of God, we would have a loved one who could watch over him and have a voice in his care. He was admitted to that second hospital with a urinary tract infection, low oxygen levels, and dehydration. They set about providing the care that he needed. I breathed a huge sigh of relief with the hospital change and the communication that came with it. This was the first miracle that the Lord brought into the situation ... at least the first that I recognized. I did not realize at that time that we still had many difficult weeks ahead of us. This was October 31.

At the new hospital, my daughter was able to go in and wash his face, wet his lips, and speak to him. At this point, he could do little more than open his eyes and look at her. They set about inserting a feeding tube to provide nourishment. Until that time, he had only had IV fluids. His blood pressure was highly elevated and he was on oxygen. He did continue to suffer with some of the delirium during this time. He was also stubborn with the hospital staff and very uncomfortable. The beautiful part of the new situation was that we were blessed to have my daughter there speaking life over him and to his caretakers. The other staff knew that he was her grandfather, and she would tell them that he was an active, independent, and highly intelligent man who lived alone, walked his dogs, and lived a good and healthy life. This helped them to see beyond the state he appeared to be in at the time. One night, I spoke with a friend, a woman of faith and a strong prayer warrior for many years. She prayed over

Your New IDENTITY

the phone with me. She was led by the Spirit of God to not only pray for his health, but to pray for emotional heart healing from things stemming from his childhood. We both had peace after those prayers. This was November 13.

That very next day I knew that I had witnessed God work a miracle. That morning Dad was sitting up, and my daughter did a FaceTime call with my dad, myself, and my siblings. He was emotional and full of joy. It blew my mind when he said during that call, "I love my sister," referring to a sister he'd been estranged from since the loss of my grandma six years earlier. Not only had the Lord done a miracle with his physical health, He had also done a miracle in heart healing. After more than twenty days in intensive care, this was the first day of his recovery process. This was November 14.

In quick succession came the steps to his recovery. The feeding tube was removed and he began to eat. He asked for a razor and his toothbrush. He was moved to a floor where we could come and bring him food. We were able to visit him for the first time on his seventieth birthday on November 17. By Thanksgiving he was moved to a rehab facility and was able to come home on December 3 after thirty-seven days in the hospital. He continued his rehab efforts and was in tip-top condition in no time.

After his initial recovery, my daughter told me, "Mom, I didn't know how to tell you, but I didn't think he was going to make it out of there." She told me that his condition was worse than I'd known and that most patients don't make it once they have reached the point he'd gotten to.

My dad would soon tell me that he believes he came out of the experience healthier than he'd been before. He has a restored relationship with his sister. He believes that he was the recipient of a miracle. He knows he was.

God is still on the throne. He is still doing miracles and healing and answering prayers. The Bible tells us that He is the same yesterday, today, and always. Hallelujah for that!

Abundant Life

We are forgiven, yet often we hold on to our past failures and behavior. Christ died to set us free from these things. It is up to us to let go and walk in our newfound freedom. After all, we wouldn't intentionally live as though His torturous death on the cross was in vain. Not a single believer would want Jesus to have died in vain. The life of a Christian should bring glory to God. The Bible tells us that Christ came to bring us life, and that we may have it more abundantly. Abundant love, abundant joy, abundant faith, abundant wisdom, and abundant provision. Abundance in this world and in eternity.

> The thief does not come, except to steal and kill and destroy. I came that they may have life, and that they may have it more abundantly.
> (John 10:10)

How glorious is a God who saves me from the depth of my mess, cleans me up, redeems me, and calls me His own? All praise to You, my Lord. All praise to You!!

Chapter 7

The Trinity

As discussed in a previous chapter, we have been created as a spirit who possesses a soul and lives in a physical body in this world. Our three-part nature reflects the image of our triune God. Notice how God self-refers in a plural fashion in Scripture:

> Then God said, "Let us make man in our image, after our likeness, and let them have dominion over the fish of the sea, and over the birds of the air, and over the livestock, and over all the earth and over every creeping thing that creeps on the earth." (Genesis 1:26)

Our God possesses a triune nature that is often referred to as the Trinity. These are three distinct personalities working intricately as one Godhead: the Father, the Son, and the Holy Spirit.

> In the beginning was the Word, and the Word was with God, and the Word was God. He was in the beginning with God. All things were

> created through Him, and without Him nothing
> was created that was created. (John 1:1–3)

Years ago I heard the Trinity explained like this: Think of God as the sun (the source). Think of the light that we see coming from the sun as the Son (Jesus, the Word) and think of the heat, warmth, and light that we experience from the sun as the Holy Spirit. This vivid illustration has stuck with me. It's a striking aid in understanding how three can exist at the same time individually and as one.

> The Word became flesh and dwelt among us,
> and we saw His glory, the glory as the only
> Son of the Father, full of grace and truth. (John 1:14)

Holy Spirit, light my path and guide my feet so that my ways will be Your ways and You will be glorified through me.

Chapter 8

Relationship

> But let him who glories glory in this, that he understands and knows Me, that I am the Lord who exercises lovingkindness, justice, and righteousness in the earth. For in these things I delight, says the Lord. (Jeremiah 9:24)

Our Creator wants a relationship with us. His Spirit is with us always and dwells within us. He doesn't relate to us at arm's length or just as the distant recipient of a prayer. He is not a God who is far off and untouchable. He delights in being a part of each of our days and a part of our decisions. He wants us to turn to Him in our good times and in our trials.

Scripture tells us that when Jesus died, the veil of the temple was torn from top to bottom. This veil separated the main part of the temple (where men were) from the area where the high priest would stand before the Lord and make atonement for our sins. Prior to this time, only the high priest could enter the area separated by the veil. The priest would enter once a year to make atonement for the sins of Israel. The tearing of the veil on the day that Christ died on the cross is very significant. It represented the birth of a path to a new relationship, a relationship in which believers can come directly before God through Jesus and His sacrifice. We no longer need any man (i.e., priest) to be a mediator for us. Christ is worthy and makes us worthy to petition God ourselves through His name.

Relationship vs. Religion

Often when you hear believers refer to the difference between relationship and religion, it is because they recognize that some of the man-made traditions, doctrines, and theories that are handed down aren't in line with the intention of the Word. Probably every denomination has some form of tradition that is not necessary for a relationship with God. We find comfort in tradition and habits, don't we?

If you are not maintaining a close relationship with the Lord there is a chance of falling into legalism. Legalism is a rigid religious mindset that insinuates that we earn and keep our salvation by our own hand and efforts (i.e., works). This is a dangerous thought process because nothing we can do or say can *earn* salvation. To say that our own behavior or acts earn salvation is like stating that we don't need the sacrifice Jesus made at the cross and His subsequent resurrection. It is like saying that His sacrifice at the cross was unnecessary or in vain.

There is also danger in putting faith in a man-made organized religion or denomination, because anything man-made is temporary. A church or leader may stray from the path, causing them to fail. Putting our faith in the wrong place can cause us heartbreak, disillusionment, and even the shipwreck of our faith if something goes south. So, we put our faith in Jesus. When our faith is placed on the foundation of Scripture and relationship, we can recognize a disappointing situation for what it is, human imperfection. And we can stay strong, shake off the disappointment, and stay on our path of faith.

The enemy is quick to take advantage of dependence on religion and insert confusion in his efforts to mislead the people of God. This is why a strong relationship with God and digging into His Word for yourself on any given subject is desirable and, in fact, crucial.

Judging Others

During the final drafting of this book, the Lord moved my heart to insert a bit about judgment. Judging others impacts our relationships with fellow Christians and with God Himself. Judgment of others can be a common pitfall for mature Christians, those who have come to think they "have it all together" or that they certainly know the truth about any bit of doctrine. This is an easy bump to hit because we don't really have to veer off of our path to hit it. It is more of a side issue, right? But when we judge others, it actually puts us in a dangerous place in our walk with Christ. We do not really know what He is working on in other people's lives. And I would venture to say that our uncharitable judgment may very well be a worse problem than whatever we are judging in others. Judgment of others is sneaky. We tend to clothe it in little comments to other believers about that person struggling or needing prayer—a Christian form of gossip, if you will. Bottom line. Steer clear of judging fellow Christians and their walk with God. If you find judgment rearing its ugly head, pray. Give it to the Lord. Ask Him to remove it from your life. Always remember that Jesus did not walk among the Pharisees, who believed that they were "holier than thou," and above it all, He came for the lost. You cannot be a light to anyone if you are judging them. As I

> *When we judge others, it actually puts us in a dangerous place in our walk with Christ.*

put these words to paper, the Spirit of God impresses me with the subject's gravity by how quickly and with what strength I am able to express these thoughts.

> Do not judge, or you too will be judged. For in the same way you judge others, you will be judged, and with the measure you use, it will be measured to you. (Matthew 7: 1–2 NIV)

Chapter 9

Praise

> Make a joyful noise unto the Lord, all the earth!
> Serve the Lord with gladness; come before
> His presence with singing. Know that the Lord,
> He is God. It is He who has made us, and
> not we ourselves; we are His people and the
> sheep of His pasture. Enter into His gates with
> thanksgiving, and into His courts with praise;
> be thankful to Him, and bless His name. For
> the Lord is good; His mercy endures forever,
> and His faithfulness to all generations.
> (Psalm 100:1–5)

Praise is an act of submission, adoration, appreciation, and thanksgiving. The Bible tells us that God inhabits our praise. It draws His Spirit to us and brings us into His presence. Our praise is a sweet fragrance to Him. Once we learn to recognize God's work and movement in our lives, praise will begin to bubble up inside us. It is difficult to hide the thanksgiving and joy that come from the influence of God moving in our lives. When we begin to realize how far we come from where we were without Him, there will be joyful tears and moments when we fall to our knees in gratitude.

> Let everything that has breath praise the Lord.
> Praise the Lord! (Psalm 150:6)

Praise in Song
We sing songs of praise, songs of mercy, songs of thanksgiving, songs celebrating our salvation. We praise with our voices, we praise with instruments, we praise with shouts of joy and enthusiasm. We move, we clap, we sway, we dance. Sometimes we cry.

Praise in Word
We tell the Lord of His greatness, mercy, and faithfulness. We tell Him that we love Him. We speak to others of the good He has done for us in our lives and the lives of those we love.

Praise in Submission
We show praise in submitting to His ways and putting our fleshly ways under our feet, in living a sanctified life, in bowing before Him, lifting our hands to Him. By obedience to the Word and to what He puts on our hearts. Giving ourselves over to Him in mind, body, and spirit.

Praise in Tithing and Giving

We show praise to God through tithing and giving. The word "tithe" in Hebrew means a tenth. We don't give God the leftovers; we give him the first fruits, the cream off the top, the first ten percent of the bounty. He then blesses the remainder and rebukes the devourer.

It is most beneficial to view each and every good thing that comes our way as belonging to God, because it does. When we understand that everything is His, and we are only given stewardship over it in this world, it will be much easier to part with it as He wills. When we understand that everything belongs to the Lord, we can best and most obediently give His ten percent back to Him.

> *We show praise in submitting to His ways, in living a sanctified life in bowing before Him.*

> Bring all the tithes into the storehouse, that there may be food in My house, and test Me now in this, says the Lord of Hosts, if I will not open for you the windows of heaven and pour out for you a blessing, that there will not be room enough to receive it. I will rebuke the devourer for your sakes, so that it will not

> destroy the fruit of your ground, and the vines
> in your field will not fail to bear fruit, says the
> LORD of Hosts. Then all the nations will call you
> blessed, for you will be a delightful land, says
> the LORD of Hosts. (Malachi 3:10–12)

Notice that God actually says "test Me" in this verse. That sounds like an invitation.

It is easy to see this only as it pertains to financial tithing and giving. But it is so much more than that. We not only tithe ten percent of our income, but of our time, energy, talents, and other resources as well.

The verse says that He will open the windows of heaven and pour out a blessing that we will not even have room enough to receive. This tells me that, if I make time for Him, He will bless me with time. If I use my talents for Him, He will bless those talents. I don't know about you, but this seems like a pretty good deal!

Praise in Action

We show praise by the way we live our lives each day. We praise God with our integrity, we praise Him with our honesty, and we praise Him in the love that we show to others. We praise Him when we demonstrate the fruits of the Spirit in our lives and to others. We praise Him when we tithe and give financially to His kingdom. We praise Him when we treat everything that He has given to us with good stewardship, whether our home, our possessions, the people He has put in our lives, or our finances. We praise Him when we teach and lead others in His ways. We praise Him by the way we treat our spouse and by the way we raise our children. We praise Him by how we conduct ourselves in our jobs or in our careers. We even praise Him when we practice self-care, both emotionally and in our health and our hygiene.

Let everything I do exalt You, Lord. Let me give glory to You in all You have trusted in me. Let me recognize always that all good things come from You and act accordingly!! Amen!!

Chapter 10

Armor

> Finally, my brothers, be strong in the Lord and in the power of His might. Put on the whole armor of God that you may be able to stand against the schemes of the devil. For our fight is not against flesh and blood, but against principalities, against powers, against the rulers of the darkness of this world, and against spiritual forces of evil in the heavenly places. (Ephesians 6:10–12)
>
> Therefore, take up the whole armor of God that you may be able to resist in the evil day, and having done all, to stand. (Ephesians 6:13)

A believer comes to the battles set before him strengthened by the weapons of his or her faith. We fight and defend with the belt of truth around our waist. We defend ourselves with the breastplate of righteousness against the accusations of the enemy and the world. We walk our paths with our feet fitted with

Your New IDENTITY

the shoes of readiness. Our shield is our faith, and we battle forward with confidence, wearing our helmet of salvation and using the sword of the Spirit and Word of God to conquer our enemy with our strength in the Lord and prayer.

> Stand therefore, having your waist girded with truth, having put on the breastplate of righteousness, having your feet fitted with the readiness of the gospel of peace, and above all, taking the shield of faith, with which you will be able to extinguish all the fiery arrows of the evil one. Take the helmet of salvation and the sword of the Spirit, which is the word of God. (Ephesians 6:14–17)

We rise each morning and spiritually dress for the day in praise, prayer, and by putting on the armor of God. This is especially effective when we are walking through the valleys of our lives. Gird up your loins in the strength of the Lord and hand Him the reins!!

> Pray in the Spirit always with all kinds of prayer and supplication. To that end be alert with all perseverance and supplication for all the saints. (Ephesians 6:18)

As a new creation we are no longer to live in the ways of a fallen man in a fallen world. We know that our battle is fought on our knees, and we have a direct access and relationship with the Victor Himself.

> And then all this assembly will know that it is not by sword and spear that the LORD saves. For the battle belongs to the LORD, and He will give you into our hands. (1 Samuel 17:47)

Thank You, dear Lord, that when I stand with You, I stand on the side of victory and righteousness. I cast my cares on You and You are ever faithful and just to fight my battles for me. Hallelujah, Lord of Hosts, and glory to Your name forever!!!

We know that our battle is fought on our knees, and we have a direct access and relationship with the Victor Himself.

Chapter 11

Prayer

> Therefore pray in this manner: Our Father who is in heaven, hallowed be Your name. Your kingdom come; Your will be done on earth, as it is in heaven. Give us this day our daily bread. And forgive us our debts, as we forgive our debtors. And lead us not into temptation, but deliver us from evil. For Yours is the kingdom and the power and the glory forever. Amen.
> (Matthew 6:9–13)

Jesus showed us prayer by example, praising the Father, confessing His will and glory. His prayer acknowledges that God supplies our needs from His riches in glory and forgives us each day for our sins and iniquities as we walk in forgiveness of our brothers and sisters. Our Lord models the plea for God's protection as He keeps our path straight.

Jesus illustrates how we enter the courts and come into the presence of God through praise. He shows us that it is fitting to begin our prayers by praising Him and coming before Him.

> Enter into His gates with thanksgiving, and into His courts with praise; be thankful to Him, and bless His name. (Psalm 100:4)

Jesus prays, "Your will be done, on earth as it is in heaven." It might be tempting when we are praying to tell God how to do His job. For instance, when we pray for someone's salvation, to suggest to Him the different ways He can reach that person. Or when we have a need, letting Him know the different avenues He could take to fill that need. While God knows our heart ... and may even be amused by our eagerness to help, it is not necessary to give Him the instruction. He knit every one of us in our mother's womb. He knows us inside and out and knows our nature far better than we ever could know ourselves. This is true not only for us ... but for our loved ones for whom we are standing in prayer and intervention. Perhaps in some situations it is as simple as praying God's will over a situation. His will is perfect.

Faith is knowing that our prayers are answered. Wisdom knows that sometimes the answer is no.

Some of the most powerful prayers might be rooted in words right from the Bible. Find Scriptures to support your prayers and then paraphrase, using your own words: "Lord, we know that it is not Your will that anyone should perish." "Father, we know that You knit us in our mother's womb and know the very number of hairs on our heads."

> You brought my inner parts into being; You wove me in my mother's womb.
> (Psalm 139:13)

> Are not five sparrows sold for two pennies? Yet not one of them is forgotten by God. Indeed, even the hairs of your head are all numbered. Therefore do not fear. You are more valuable than many sparrows. (Luke 12:6–7)

Faith is knowing that our prayers are answered. Wisdom knows that sometimes the answer is no.

Using Jesus' example of prayer, a prayer may look something like this:

Address Him: *Dear Father or Dear Lord,*

Enter into His presence with praise and adoration: *You are a good and worthy Father; You are King of Kings and Lord of Lords. Your name is worthy of glory and honor and praise. You are a merciful God, full of kindness and grace.*

Petition Him for the right heart: *Lord, give me the eyes to see others as You see them. Give me the heart to meet them where they are. Give me the words to speak Your will and the wisdom to see clearly.*

Pray for others: *Father, I pray that You meet them where they are. You created them. You know them inside and out. Turn their hardened hearts to flesh. Open their eyes to see the truth. Holy Spirit, speak to their spirits.*

Pray for His perfect will to be done in any situation: *Father, You know the best outcome for this situation. Only You can see the ultimate and unquestionably best outcome. I know that You are able to turn every situation to work it out for the good.*

Give thanks before Him: *Lord, I am so thankful for the mighty work of salvation that You did at the cross. I thank You for all the blessings and gifts that You have given me and continue to give. I know that everything that is good is a gift from You, God. And I am humbly grateful for Your perfect gifts.*

Oh, heavenly Father, You are faithful in Your word and in Your love for me. I honor You forever and ever!

Chapter 12

Names of God

> Therefore, My people shall know My name;
> therefore, they shall know in that day that I am
> He who does speak: Here I am. (Isaiah 52:6)

Our creator has a name, and He has many names. Although He is God Almighty, His actual name is not God (with a capital G to differentiate from all the "gods" of this world). His many names speak to the multiple facets of His personality. We may call Him Abba (our Father) when we speak to Him in personal intimacy. Here are some other examples of the names of God.

- **El Shaddai ... Lord God Almighty**

  This name speaks of His ultimate power over all and refers to Jacob's revelation of God.

- **El Elyon ... The Most High God**

  God is mighty and strong.

Your New IDENTITY

- **Adonai ... Lord, Master**

  You will see this in the Bible as Lord, in lower-case to distinguish it from Yahweh. This is, perhaps, a less formal name than Yahweh, and a name we might use reflecting our submission to Him.

- **Yahweh ... Lord, Jehovah**

  This is the proper name of God. When you see Lord in all capital letters in the English translation, it is referring to Yahweh. This is the revelation of Moses when God reveals, "I AM WHO I AM" (Exodus 3:14). It refers to the closeness and intimacy to God. Yahweh brings deliverance, forgiveness, and guidance.

- **Yahweh/Jehovah Nissi ... The Lord My Banner**

  We stand behind His name. He goes before us in battle. He truly is our victory.

- **Yahweh/Jehovah Rohi ... The Lord Ny Shepherd**

  He leads us to salvation and makes straight our path.

- **Yahweh/Jehovah Rapha … The Lord That Heals**

  He heals our physical body, He heals our emotional wounds, and He restores our mind, body, and spirit.

- **Yahweh/Jehovah Shammah … The Lord Is There**

  He is present.

- **Yahweh/Jehovah Tsidkenu … The Lord Our Righteousness**

  It is not by our own work that we become righteous, but by and through Him.

- **Yahweh/Jehovah Mekoddishkem (M'Kaddesh) … The Lord Who Sanctifies You**

  He alone cleanses His people.

- **El Olam … The Everlasting God**

  God is without beginning or end. He is the Alpha and the Omega. He is the Beginning and the End.

- **Yahweh Elohim … God or Creator, Mighty and Strong**

  He spoke the world into existence and breathed life into man.

- **Yahweh-Elohim ... Lord God**

  A combination of His unique and proper name, Yahweh (LORD) and His more generic name, Elohim, which combination signifies that He is Lord of Lords.

- **Yahweh/Jehovah Jireh ... The Lord Will Provide**

  Every good thing comes from Him.

- **Yahweh/Jehovah Shalom ... The Lord Is Peace; Everlasting God**

  In Him we find rest and peace. The battle belongs to Him.

- **El Roi ... God of Seeing**

  He appears to His people.

- **El Gibhor ... Mighty God**

  He is bigger than any situation and above any enemy. The Author and Creator of it all.

- **Yahweh/Jehovah Sabaoth ... The Lord of Hosts**

  Hosts are of both angels and men, dwelling in both heaven and earth, Jews and Gentiles, rich and poor, master and slave.

Names of God

> For unto us a child is born, unto us a son is given, and the government shall be upon his shoulder. And his name shall be called Wonderful Counselor, Mighty God, Eternal Father, Prince of Peace. (Isaiah 9:6)

My God, Your name is above all names. You are worthy of glory and honor and praise forever.

Chapter 13

Maturity in Christ

> As newborn babies, desire the pure milk of the word, that by it you may grow, if it is true that you have experienced that the Lord is good. (1 Peter 2:2–3)

> Everyone who lives on milk is unskilled in the word of righteousness, for he is a baby. But solid food belongs to those who are mature, for those who through practice have powers of discernment that are trained to distinguish good from evil. (Hebrews 5:13–14)

Growth and maturity in your Christian walk will come by hearing the Word of God and by spending time in prayer and praise with Him. As we grow, we learn. As infants are not expected to clean up after themselves, or know when to hush, new believers have grace in their walk and learning of righteousness. However, when we have continued to grow and learn, the expectations for our walk also grow. Just as infant behaviors are no longer acceptable for a child that can walk and talk and understand what is appropriate or inappropriate, our life patterns as maturing Christians should reflect our walk with Christ. This continues throughout our journey. A mature adult should behave differently than a selfish teen.

> Your word is a lamp to my feet and a light to my path. (Psalm 119:105)

The Word of God is nourishment to our souls. Reading, studying, and hearing the words of the Bible are the ways we will grow in our walk with God. You will find a new understanding now as a believer. The Holy Spirit helps to bring the Word to life as you read and develop. As you grow, Scripture will come to life and reveal more truth and depth to you than the simple words on paper. This growth and learning will continue through your Christian walk, as there is more to know than we will have time to learn in our lifetime in this world.

> Your words were found and I ate them. And Your word became to me the joy and rejoicing of my heart, for I am called by Your name, O Lord, God of hosts. (Jeremiah 15:16)

> But He answered, "It is written, 'Man shall not live by bread alone, but by every word that

> proceeds out of the mouth of God.'"
> (Matthew 4:4)

We hear Scriptures in sermons, we read Scriptures in books, and we hear Scriptures in praise and worship songs. Our faith grows as we hear the Scriptures over and over and over again. As we submerge ourselves in the Word of God, we grow. As we grow, we see our fruits develop and mature.

Dear Father, give me wisdom and develop me into the creature that You mean for me to be.

Chapter 14

Power

There is power in the Word. The words of the Bible are commonly referred to as the "living Word." This is because a verse may speak differently to us depending on what we need from it at any given time. While the Word of God never waivers, it does remain fresh and alive and able to meet us in our circumstance.

> The word of God is alive, and active, and sharper than any two-edged sword, piercing even to the division of soul and spirit, of joints and marrow, and able to judge the thoughts and intents of the heart. (Hebrews 4:12)

Few Christians realize the power of their own words. We have been made in the very image of God, who spoke this world into existence, who has the power of life and death in His breath. We either speak forth blessings or

While the Word of God never waivers, it does remain fresh and alive and able to meet us in our circumstance.

we speak forth curses. Just as our words loose God's angels and give them permission to move in our lives and on our behalf, our words can also loose Satan's fallen angels and give them permissions with our negative or cursing words ... permissions that we do not want to give them. Angels don't intrude on our free will; we give them permission with the words that we speak over our life, circumstances, loved ones, etc. We have the ability to open and close doors in the spirit realm with our words. Speak blessings of life and love over everything and everyone in your life.

We live in a God-given freedom of choice. God does not force His will upon us. We accept salvation; it is not put on us against our will. We must ask for it, and then we receive.

Watch your tongue. Watch the words that you listen to and allow into your ears. They matter.

It is worth repeating that we mature in our faith through praise, prayer, and through the Word of God. We grow and deepen the relationship with our triune God, the Father, Son, and Holy Spirit, as we spend time in relationship and allow His influence and sanctification in our lives.

Reveal Yourself every day, dear Father. Grow me, develop me, teach me Your ways! Only You are worthy of glory, honor, and praise. Only You!

Chapter 15

Sanctification

> I am confident of this very thing, that He who began a good work in you will perfect it until the day of Jesus Christ. (Philippians 1:6)

Make no bones about it, we may come to the Lord as we are, but we won't stay that way. Accepting Jesus as our Savior is only the beginning of a life-long journey. We are born again, and thus will grow, develop, and mature in our new-found life.

While all believers who have made Christ their Lord will be on a path to sanctification, each believer will go through the process at a different pace. Our faith-walks are each personal, intimate, and unique. While there are believers who see radical and immediate transformation and deliverance from addiction and circumstance, for others it is a lengthier journey.

The speed of our sanctification is determined by so many things. Where did we start from in our lives? Did we grow up in church? Did we come from an agnostic family, or another background or belief system that was not built and centered on Christ? The length of the journey will also depend on everyone's weaknesses, strengths, personal temptations, or "trouble areas." It will depend on how much time we spend with Him in prayer, study, and quiet time. Are we willing to be obedient to the things that the Lord puts on our heart to work on? Sometimes we can simply be stubborn and willful and resistant to submitting. The good news is that we don't have to do this alone and without help. We can simply hand it over to the Lord and ask Him for the strength, wisdom, and guidance to overcome. As sanctification comes along for each of us at a different pace, it also is continuous throughout our lives. We won't reach full sanctification in this world.

Once we recognize sin in our lives, or have a new revelation of iniquity, we simply turn from that way, repent, and move forward in a new direction in that area. One more step toward our sanctification. The process isn't always fun or easy. Sometimes we struggle to hold on to our old ways ... making the lessons more difficult. But growth and rejoicing can be found just on the other side, so the result is well worth the effort.

> By this we know that we love the children of God: when we love God and keep His commandments. For this is the love of God, that we keep His commandments. And His

> commandments are not burdensome.
> (1 John 5:2–3)

The Lord our God is long suffering and full of grace. He knows our past and the intricate details of what makes us who we are. He knows our hurts, and desires so much to restore and heal those old wounds. His grace is perfect and is more than enough. He is patient and faithful. If you do a search for Scriptures regarding the word "faithful," you will find that most of them speak of God's faithfulness toward us. He wants us to know that He is present on our side. The Creator of all things has our back. This is huge.

> The Lord is not slow concerning His promise, as some count slowness. But He is patient with us, because He does not want any to perish, but all to come to repentance. (2 Peter 3:9)

We should, however, be cautioned not to take the grace of God for granted. Openness to His correction and direction in our lives is part of the relationship. The Word states that the wages of sin is death. Keep in mind that Satan and his fallen angels believe in God, and we know where they stand. We can't just ignore the part of the process that includes repentance and making Jesus our Lord. All too often we focus on the warm and fuzzy words and don't take heed of the ones we would rather all too conveniently ignore. We don't do ourselves any favors by living our lives as toddlers.

> For the wages of sin is death, but the gift of God is eternal life through Jesus Christ our Lord. (Romans 6:23)
>
> What does it profit, my brothers, if a man says he has faith but has no works? Can faith save him? If a brother or sister is naked and lacking daily food, and one of you says to them, "Depart in peace, be warmed and filled," and yet you give them nothing that the body needs, what does it profit? So faith by itself, if it has no works, is dead.
>
> But a man may say, "You have faith and I have works." Show me your faith without your works, and I will show you my faith by my works. You believe that there is one God; you do well. The demons also believe and tremble. But do you want to be shown, O foolish man, that faith without works is dead? (James 2:14–20)
>
> Therefore we should be more attentive to what we have heard, lest we drift away. (Hebrews 2:1)

Sanctification

As born-again believers, we praise, pray, and allow sanctification in our lives because we want to. Our soul is hungry for the bread of knowledge and things of God. Because we love God, we love Jesus, and we love the Holy Spirit. We recognize that we are lost and are nothing without our Creator. We see where we were without Him, and subsequently, the freedom, joy, and all the fruits of the Spirit that we have in Him. We realize truth and hope. We walk with Him and thank Him for refining us into sanctification. We trust His process.

> I counsel you to buy from Me gold refined by fire, that you may be rich, and white garments, that you may be dressed, that the shame of your nakedness may not appear, and anoint your eyes with eye salve, that you may see. Those whom I love, I rebuke and discipline. Therefore be zealous and repent. Listen! I stand at the door and knock. If anyone hears My voice and opens the door, I will come in and dine with him, and he with Me.
> (Revelation 3:18–20)

Your New IDENTITY

All praise and glory to the Lord our God who is, was, and always will be, and who redeemed us and washed us in the blood of the Lamb.

Chapter 16

The Great Commission

> Then Jesus came and spoke to them, saying, "All authority has been given to Me in heaven and on earth. Go therefore and make disciples of all nations, baptizing them in the name of the Father and of the Son and of the Holy Spirit, teaching them to observe all things I have commanded you. And remember, I am with you always, even to the end of the age." Amen.
> (Matthew 28:18–20)

As disciples of Christ Jesus, our job, our commission, our command, our duty, is to communicate the truth of Scripture and the message of salvation. This is what you will hear referred to as "the Great Commission." In our new life as disciples of Christ we are responsible to share the great good news.

Remember the ABCs of Salvation that were mentioned in a previous chapter; salvation is as simple as ABC. Re-visit that chapter to refresh your memory and keep it in your heart. Our job is easy. Use Scriptures as led by the Holy Spirit. Speak freedom and salvation and let the Holy Spirit take it from there. We may be just planting a seed, or watering a seed that was planted previously. The Holy Spirit will make sure that the seed is nurtured.

When we share the gospel (the good news), we may be tempted to turn a conversation into a debate; but be clear that it is not our responsibility to argue about the subject or to have heated debates. We present the Truth. The Holy Spirit does the work to ignite the Word in the hearer's heart, to convict the heart to confirm that they are hearing Truth, and to finish that work, water that seed, and convert that soul.

> The Lord is not slow concerning His promise, as some count slowness. But He is patient with us, because He does not want any to perish, but all to come to repentance. (2 Peter 3:9)

We may walk away from a conversation or encounter not ever knowing how it turns out in the long run. That is okay. If we are obedient to speak when the Holy Spirit prompts us, we have done our part. Scripture tells us that it is not God's desire that anyone should perish, but that each of us would have everlasting life. He knows what to do specifically to reach each heart.

The Great Commission

> He [Jesus] said to them, "Go into all the world, and preach the gospel to every creature. He who believes and is baptized will be saved. But he who does not believe will be condemned. These signs will accompany those who believe: In My name they will cast out demons; they will speak with new tongues; they will take up serpents; if they drink any deadly thing, it will not hurt them; they will lay hands on the sick, and they will recover." (Mark 16:15–18)

Sometimes He may prompt us to pray for the person on various occasions after a conversation, even weeks or months later. We can trust that the Holy Spirit is at work and when He begins a work, He is faithful to completion.

> I am confident of this very thing, that He who began a good work in you will perfect it until the day of Jesus Christ. (Philippians 1:6)

Conclusion

Receiving salvation is just the beginning of your journey. As a new creature in Christ and a baby Christian, you are only getting started. This book is merely a compilation of some basics to help you on your new walk as a believer, a resource to draw from when you hear believers use otherwise unfamiliar terms or references.

Believe that the Word contains more depth and mystery than you will discover in a lifetime. Believe that it can reveal more power and wisdom than you can imagine as you learn God's truth and experience His presence. This is just the milk. Wait until you get to the meat!

> Oh, taste and see that the Lord is good;
> Blessed is the man who takes refuge in Him.
> (Psalm 34:8)

Men and women of God have written countless books focused on the various subject matters introduced on these pages. Dig in, read, study, and grow. Seek and you will find. There is no limit to the learning and growth. As you grow in your Christian life, the Lord will use you more and more to spread His Word, nurture and serve His ministry, and guide your family and friends to find salvation. As Scripture says, the work is plentiful and the workers are few. If you are willing, He will put you to work.

As you branch out in your learning, check any new information against Scripture and ask the Holy Spirit for discernment. This will keep you from straying from the truth. Amir Tsarfati writes in his book *Revealing Revelation*, "When our beliefs and reality converge, it is reality that wins out." From time to time you will come across religious or man-made doctrine that doesn't sit right with your spirit. Continue to test these things against the Word of God and don't fret. As you continue to read Scripture and stay close to the Holy Spirit, He will correct you as you learn and grow.

Holy, holy, holy is the Lord God Almighty. Thank You, Lord, for Your words and wisdom. Thank You, Lord, for Your faithfulness!

> The LORD bless you and keep you; the LORD make His face shine on you and be gracious to you; the LORD turn his face toward you and give you peace. (Numbers 6:24–26 NIV)

Conclusion

Jesus, in You I am not a statistic.
In You I have overcome the odds
Nothing and no one could have saved me, except You.
You loved me enough to be my Savior.
You cherished me enough to pull me from darkness.
In You I am free from the guilt, darkness,
and condemnation of the world.
In You I have a new story.
In You I sing a new song.
You love me in my darkest moment and
delight with me in the light of Your love.
Jesus, in You I am found and redeemed.

Inspired to, and put to paper by, Kim Wampler-Hill

Your New IDENTITY

Dear friend,

If your spirit was stirred or touched by the contents of this book and you have not yet accepted Christ as your savior, rest assured, happening across and reading this book is not an accident. Jesus is knocking at the door and all you have to do is to open it. Jesus says in Scripture, "Listen! I stand at the door and knock. If anyone hears My voice and opens the door, I will come in and dine with him, and he with Me. To him who overcomes will I grant to sit with Me on My throne, as I also overcame and sat down with My Father on His throne" (Revelation 3:20–21).

Or perhaps you grew up in faith but have slipped into living life on your own path or fallen into the ways of the world, and you feel that tugging of the Holy Spirit coaxing you back into a relationship with Him. Either way, you can say this prayer right now. Say it out loud, confessing with your tongue:

Jesus, I believe in You. I confess that I am a sinner. I believe that You came to earth as flesh and died on the cross, shedding Your blood as the perfect sacrifice so that I can be washed clean from my sin and bondage. I accept that sacrifice as payment of my debt of sin. I choose today to make You the Lord of my life. In Jesus' name I pray, Amen!

Conclusion

Congratulations, friend! Having said this prayer, you now have a new life and a fresh start. You now have access to a whole new wonderful world. But let's not stop at that. Let's invite the Holy Spirit to baptize you:

Holy Spirit, wash over me. I welcome You into every day of my life. Guide me, teach me, lead me, and keep me. Be the light to my feet and guide to my path. When I veer to the left or the right, gently bring me back. I accept You into my life and into my heart, along with all the gifts and fruits of the Spirit that come with You. Open my eyes to truth; give me wisdom and understanding. In Jesus' mighty name, Amen.

Now read through the book again and see what you might have missed!

Dear Lord, let the words of this book bless the lives of those who read. Let it help to provide a foundation to build on. Let it glorify You and help to disciple Your people. Let the words and Scriptures within reveal Your heart for the reader. You are good through and through and worthy of all glory, honor, and praise. In the name of Jesus, Amen!

Author Bio

Kim lives with her husband Russell and their three dogs in Lawrence, Kansas. She is a 4th generation Lawrence, KS, native and lifetime resident. She has three grown children; two daughters and one son, and flock of grandchildren (five and counting).

Kim is a member of Rev City Church in Lawrence, Kansas, and where her time and talents for the church include leading small Life Groups and serving wherever needs arise.

Professionally, she has worked as a licensed insurance professional since 2000 and as a real estate agent since 2018. Together Kim and Russell run a small portfolio of apartment units and short-term rentals. They enjoy their dogs, weekends away, dinner theatre and time with family.

Kim has served on non-profit boards such as that for the local Habitat for Humanity affiliate as well as with Warm Hearts, Laura Kriz charitable fund, and a local women's networking group.

Kim is a big-picture thinker and a visionary. She sings boldly off-key, laughs at her own jokes and has an overall optimistic outlook on just about everything. One of her closest friends often jokes that she is the most cheesy person she knows and she is famous with her son-in-laws for her dad jokes, often receiving random jokes from them by text.

As a child of teen parents and a teen mother herself, Kim has overcome many obstacles and, through the grace of the Lord, lives a life of success and not as a statistic.

www.ingramcontent.com/pod-product-compliance
Lightning Source LLC
La Vergne TN
LVHW051845080426
835512LV00018B/3074